INTRODUCTION
to the
PSALMS

PARTICIPANT WORKBOOK

NEXT LEVEL
CATHOLIC

Written by Dr. Carol Younger & Matthew Leonard

Graphic Design by Patty Borgman

Next Level Catholic Academy | NextLevelCatholicAcademy.com

Table of Contents

Welcome to *Introduction to the Psalms*

Welcome to *Introduction to the Psalms*, presented by Next Level Catholic Academy.

Founded by renowned evangelist Matthew Leonard, Next Level Catholic Academy is one of the world's premiere online Catholic communities dedicated to teaching Scripture and authentic Catholic spirituality. Steeped in the tradition of saints like John of the Cross, Teresa of Avila, and Thomas Aquinas, our goal is to guide regular Catholics, step-by-step, down the path to nothing less than sainthood.

More than education, this is *transformation*!

Introduction to the Psalms is merely one of the course offerings presented by Next Level Catholic Academy. To learn more about all the courses offered and join Catholics all over the world in studying the depth and beauty of the Catholic faith, visit **NextLevelCatholicAcademy.com**.

How To Use This Workbook

Each lesson in this study contains the following sections:

+ Review of the Previous Lesson

+ Topics Covered

+ Play Video

+ Prayers Inspired by the Psalms

+ Saint Quote

+ Review of Key Content

+ Discussion Opportunities

+ Scripture for Meditation

+ Notes & Journal

How you use the sections depends completely on what works best for your needs. The written sections are there for either group or individual use. Some groups simply discuss the video and leave the journaling and other content for use outside the group. Other groups work their way through each portion as a whole group, reading the passages aloud. Again, it's up to you how you want to do it.

As you can see, we have provided Review and Discussion Questions to help spur group discussion.

Answers to the Review Questions can be found by the Leader (or other participants if they have access) by logging into their account and opening the lesson in question. (There are no answers to Discussion Questions since they are intended to be open-ended.)

Finally, don't forget that this study is a *small* portion of the rest of Next Level Catholic Academy.

For information on how to enroll in Next Level Catholic Academy and join people from all over the world in the quest for deeper understanding and practice of the Catholic spiritual life, visit **NextLevelCatholicAcademy.com**!

"Game-changer!"

"Next Level Catholic Academy is a treasure in my life!"

"This has been beyond what I ever could have imagined. So excited to learn more!"

LESSON ONE

Understanding the Psalms

"Man is in search of God. In the act of creation, God calls every being from nothingness into existence. Crowned with glory and honor, man is, after the angels, capable of acknowledging how majestic is the name of the Lord in all the earth."

(CCC 2566, CITING PSALM 8:5, 8:1)

Topics Covered

+ Popularity of the Psalms
+ Occasions for the Psalms
+ Authorship of the Psalms

+ Parallelism and the Psalms
+ Categories of Psalms

Prayers Inspired by the Psalms

Blessed be the one who delights in the law of the Lord,
praying over the will of God for his life.
That one is like a tree planted by streams of water,
a tree that gives fruit in his season of life.
The Lord knows him well,
and all of his ways God prospers.
(Adapted from Psalm 1)

"Attribute to God every good that you have received."

— ST ANTHONY OF PADUA —

Review of Key Content

1. The Hebrew word for "a psalm" is *mizmor,* which comes from a root meaning "to pluck." What does this suggest about the Psalms?

2. David wrote about half of the Psalms. Who are some other authors who made contributions to the book of Psalms?

3. When were the Psalms written? How long a period of time separates the most ancient psalm from the most recent?

Discussion Opportunities

(Share your thoughts with the group.)

1. King David was probably illiterate, yet he composed songs with melodies for religious gatherings. This might bring to mind some prayers or even some original songs you have heard in Church events. What has been your response to those?

2. Have you ever noticed that music helps you remember words? What are some songs you learned long ago that have stuck in your memory?

3. What kind of spiritual writing helps you pray and worship? Have you noticed any similarities or differences between it and the Psalms you have heard at Mass or have read for prayer?

4. What drew you to this study of Psalms? What aspect of learning about the Psalms appeals to you the most?

5. What is your motivation for undertaking this study of the Psalms? Do you have an expectation for your prayer life or spiritual growth from this study?

Write Your Word Upon My Heart

"Let what you heard from the beginning abide in you. If what you heard from the beginning abides in you, then you will abide in the Son and in the Father. And this is what he has promised us, eternal life."

1 JOHN 2:24-25

Notes & Journal

LESSON TWO

Psalms & the Big Picture of Salvation History

"In the Psalms David, inspired by the Holy Spirit, is the first prophet of Jewish and Christian prayer. The prayer of Christ, the true Messiah and Son of David, will reveal and fulfill the meaning of this prayer....The prayer at the dedication of the Temple relies on God's promise and covenant, on the active presence of his name among his People recalling his mighty deeds at the Exodus."

CCC 2579-2580

Review of the Previous Lesson

Because he probably couldn't read or write, the poet of the Psalms likely composed his poetry orally and someone else wrote it down. Even so, poetry from Psalms has such importance, and such popularity, that it is included in liturgical readings of every Mass in the Catholic Church throughout the world every day.

The major author, David, who lived in the 10th century before Jesus was born, was the youngest son of Jesse and a shepherd until God singled him out and Samuel anointed him. The Holy Spirit rushed upon David, though he was not a sinless man. David became a warrior, and then a musician in the court of King Saul. He grew into a political leader, and head of his tribe, Judah. Later he became the 2nd King of Israel, and founded an international kingdom, with Jerusalem on Mt. Zion as its capital.

David was a well-rounded man who not only mastered the art of war, but also created literature and ritual for worship, including the Psalms. Numbering 150, the Psalms are religious poetry, and have been translated into almost every human language. They remain the most popular collection of poetry ever produced. The word "psalm" comes from an ancient word in Hebrew (*mizmor*), and was eventually translated into a Greek word, *psalmos*, meaning "to pluck," referring to a plucked instrument, the lyre, which accompanied the song when sung aloud.

David wrote about half of the Psalms. He also appointed a Levitical choir called the Sons of Korah, who authored about a dozen psalms. Two of these, Heman and Ethan, each wrote a psalm (Psalms 88 and 89). A choir leader named Asaph wrote about another dozen psalms. Other authors of Psalms include David's son, Solomon (Psalm 72 and 120), and Moses (Psalm 90).

There are different categories of Psalms: laments and penitential prayers, thanksgivings and hymns, royal and Zion psalms, messianic and imprecation (curses) Psalms. The largest is laments. The second largest is thanksgiving psalms, in particular the *todah*, which gives thanks to God for deliverance.

Topics Covered

- How the Psalms fit into the Bible
- David's starring role in salvation history
- God's covenant family bond with His people
- Covenant beginnings with Adam and Noah
- Abraham and the Calvary of the Old Testament
- God's covenants with Moses and David
- The Prophets of the New Covenant

 PLAY VIDEO

Prayers Inspired by the Psalms

Give ear to my words, O Lord;

Hear me in the morning as I offer my day to You.

Because of Your Love, I will enter into your temple,

I will worship You and You alone.

Help me follow Your straight way all my life,

I will sing for joy eternally.

You are my shield and You bless me always.

(Adapted from Psalm 5)

"Understanding…consists of showing why there are a number of covenants with mankind and in teaching what is the character of those covenants."

— ST. IRENAEUS OF LYONS —

Review of Key Content

1. Can you name the six major covenants in salvation history covered in Lesson Two?

2. What is your understanding of where the Psalms fit in the story of the covenants?

3. Of the five mountains presented in our summary of biblical history (i.e. Eden, Moriah, Ararat, Sinai, and Zion), which one has been the most emphasized in homilies, sermons, RCIA, or other instances where you have heard these stories of covenants? Which one were you the most familiar with? Are any of them totally new to you?

4. According to the video, which two mountains had rivers flowing from them? What was the significance of the rivers on those two mountains?

5. What's so important about the Tree of Life and the River of Life in Eden? What gift did they impart?

6. Do you remember the word for "perfect peace" in Hebrew?

7. Name some similarities between the attempted-sacrifice of Isaac and the sacrifice of Christ.

Discussion Opportunities

(Share your thoughts with the group.)

1. Covenant as family bond is formed by an oath. Think about a Baptism or adoption ceremony you know about or have attended. What struck you as important for parents? The baby crying as the water was poured, or the child and parents standing in front of the judge? What internal thoughts or prayers might the parents have had?

2. Though God restores "family relationship" in His covenant with Noah, there remained a lack of "shalom" (perfect peace) because of sin. In your family experience, what sacrifices are needed to maintain family relationships? What are the results when sacrifices are not made?

3. Communication makes or breaks relationships. Can you think of a "Tower of Babel" incident in your family or workplace where people stopped communicating and became alienated from one another? What was the source of these tensions, and how were they resolved?

4. Does gaining a greater understanding of Salvation History and the gift of your Faith prompt you to make any changes in your Catholic practice?

Write Your Word Upon My Heart

 "But to all who received him, who believed in his name, he gave power to become children of God; who were born, not of blood nor of the will of the flesh nor of the will of man, but of God. And the Word became flesh and dwelt among us...."

JOHN 1:12-14

Notes & Journal

LESSON THREE

Picturing the Psalms & the Kingdom of David

"The king lifts his hands toward heaven and begs the Lord, on his own behalf, on behalf of the entire people, and of the generations yet to come, for the forgiveness of their sins and for their daily needs, so that the nations may know that He is the only God and that the heart of his people may belong wholly and entirely to him."

CCC 2580

Review of Previous Lesson

The Psalms are part of the large biblical story from Genesis to Revelation. David, the author of a large portion of the Psalms, is also part of that larger story that begins with Adam and climaxes in the unveiling of the New Creation heralded in Revelation.

The Covenant is the critical glue of the whole Bible narrative. This is presented in the drawings of the Adamic, Noahic, Abrahamic, Mosaic, Davidic and Eucharistic covenants. Adam is found near the Tree of Life on Mt. Eden from which flows the River of Life.

Upon landing on Mt. Ararat after 40 days and nights on the ark, Noah and his family reboot the Creation covenant. Abraham and his son Isaac cooperate in the Calvary of the Old Testament on a chain of mountains in Moriah (the site later known as Mt. Zion). Many centuries later, after enslavement by the Pharaoh in Egypt, God sends Moses to lead out all Israel (Jacob's 12 sons/tribes) to their own land in Canaan, making a family covenant with them along the way.

Humanity continued to sin, including the Prophet leader Moses. Centuries passed again. After the royal failure of Saul, Israel receives King David, a very unique individual, in whom the Holy Spirit powerfully moved. It is he who creates the Psalms. David's covenant is given on Mt. Zion, including new worship, a Temple, and dynastic heirs continuing for centuries.

However, following David and his son Solomon (who had his own issues), most of the descendant kings were quite sinful. During this time, God sent prophets (e. g., Isaiah, Jeremiah, Ezekiel) who brought both bad and good news. The bad news was Israel's sin would bring punishment. The good news promised a new and perfect King, as well as a new and perfect temple in the future.

The promised New Covenant is the Eucharistic Covenant; in fact, the Eucharist *is* the new covenant. Jesus forms this new covenant in the Upper Room, turning bread and wine into his Eucharistic body and blood. Jesus confirms His covenant at Calvary on his Cross. The "river" of blood and water flowing from the side of Christ are the signs of the sacraments, through which the faithful receive the Holy Spirit.

While Adam and Eve lost the Holy Spirit in Eden through sin, Christ restores this loss on Calvary. Mt. Eden and Mt. Calvary have similarities. The tree of life in Eden and the tree of life (the cross bearing the body of Christ) at Calvary are the same. The river in Eden waters the whole earth, and the river flowing from the side of Christ brings eternal life through the sacraments to all who come to the New Covenant.

The Psalms fit into this covenant history in the Davidic covenant. David prophesied the new or Eucharistic covenant in Psalms subtly. Jesus is the fulfillment of that prophecy as the Son of David. David's Psalms are ancient song and prayer for the ancient temple, a prototype of Christ's body and of the Church. The Psalms are a "river" of poetry and song that the Church enjoys from the Davidic covenant and the family relationship through David's son, our Lord Jesus Christ.

Topics Covered

- Comparison of Mosaic and Davidic Covenants
  - Location: Mt. Sinai and Mt. Zion
  - Sanctuary: Tabernacle tent and Temple stone
  - Instruction of Israel: the Law and Wisdom Literature
  - Governance: national republic and international kingdom
  - Worship: solemn silence and thanksgiving with song
  - Sacrifice: *olah* whole burnt offering and *todah* thank offering/feast
  - Function: prophet/leader and priest, prophet, king, exorcist
- The Domination of David
- Psalms as the product of the Davidic Covenant
- Eucharistic foreshadowing in the Psalms
- Overview of the Five Books of Psalms

Prayers Inspired by the Psalms

Lord, I bless you and delight in your plans for me,

And I try to walk in the way you have set for me.

My delight is to do your will,

Just as all creation follows your plan for it.

You know my ways,

Help me stand firm in your plan for me,

Let not the winds of change assault me.

Be with me, O Lord.

(Adapted from Psalm 1)

"We become what we love and who we love shapes
what we become."

— ST. CLARE OF ASSISI —

Review of Key Content

1. How many times each are Moses and David mentioned in the Old Testament?

2. Name at least three ways David is a prominent figure in the Old Testament, other than as author of the Psalms.

3. Describe the difference between the liturgy of Moses and the liturgy of David.

4. List four features of the Davidic covenant that are different from the Mosaic covenant.

5. You heard in the video that the Psalter consists of five books, and that each book has a particular "mood." Describe the mood of at least two of the five books.

Discussion Opportunities

(Share your thoughts with the group.)

1. We've learned that the New Covenant fulfills key features of the Davidic covenant. How does this fulfillment relate to matters of sacrifice and worship?

2. Do you pray the Liturgy of the Hours? If not, have you ever used the Psalms in your personal prayer? What advantages do you see in praying Psalms?

3. Do you have a favorite Psalm? Do you pray it regularly? If so, what was the effect on your relationship with God?

4. Have you ever experienced a sense of being "out in exile" like the Israelites after the collapse of the kingdom? What was your experience of prayer during that time?

Write Your Word Upon My Heart

 "I have been with you wherever you went, and have cut off all your enemies from before you; and I will make of you a great name, like the name of the great ones of the earth."

2 SAMUEL 7:9

Notes & Journal

LESSON FOUR

Entering the Double Doors – Psalms 1 & 2

"The Psalter's many forms of prayer...are a mirror of God's marvelous deeds in the history of his people, ... that can be prayed in truth by men of all times and conditions."

CCC 2588

Review of Previous Lesson

David is prominent in the biblical story of God's covenants with mankind. Statistically, he is mentioned even more frequently in the Old Testament than Moses. He is probably best known as the primary contributor to the Bible's book of prayer, the Book of Psalms. Besides being a great king who reigned over Israel's international empire, he is also a priestly and prophetic figure.

Moses and David stand out in the Old Testament as two towering figures with whom God ratified a major covenant. When we compare these two covenants, the Mosaic and Davidic, we notice 6 striking differences that give us a clue to the future direction of salvation history.

Location:	Mt. Sinai to Mt. Zion
Type of Sanctuary:	Tabernacle to Temple
Type of Instruction:	The Law to Wisdom Literature
Type of Government:	National Republic to International Empire
Type of Worship:	Silent and solemn to song and thanksgiving
Type of Sacrifice:	*Olah* (Whole burnt offering) vs *Todah* (Thank Offering)

Ultimately, Jesus comes to fulfill the Davidic Covenant, not the Mosaic. He brings us to a heavenly Zion, not a heavenly Sinai. He forms the Church, the fulfillment of

David's international kingdom. Not merely silent, the Church's liturgy is celebrated with song and Psalms, which flow from the Davidic Covenant. Christ fulfills the roles of priest, exorcist, prophet and king originally embodied in David.

The Book of Psalms is divided into five books. Book One extends from Psalm 1 to 41, and contains individual laments from the first part of David's story when he is running from King Saul's attempts on his life.

Book Two is more joyful. It extends from Psalm 42 to 72 and introduces what we call Zion Psalms, written during David's kingship over Israel, as well as the transfer of the royal crown to Solomon, his son.

Book Three, extending from Psalm 73 to 89, features communal laments and a tone of despair. It mourns the collapse of the kingdom and ensuing exile of the Israelites.

Book Four, extending from Psalm 90 to 106, is melancholy in tone. It features several psalms that review the history of Israel's relationship with the Lord.

Book Five, extending from Psalm 107 to 150, includes the Psalms of Ascent, so-called because they were sung when Israelites made a pilgrimage to the holy city of Jerusalem. Hallelujah Psalms command us to praise the Lord in the restored temple that is the destination of all the faithful worshippers of God. There the perfect king, Jesus, will reign in the perfect temple, His Mystical Body, in the heavenly Mount Zion.

Topics Covered

- ◆ Psalm 1 – God's wisdom in his law

- ◆ Psalms as a form of instruction

- ◆ Two paths of life – one destructive, one life-giving

- ◆ Psalm 2 – God's royal son, sovereign over all the earth

- ◆ Psalms as a vicarious experience of the Son of God

- ◆ Covenant language in Psalm 2

- ◆ Spiritual combat and taking refuge in God's Son

- ◆ Living daily in the presence of God

- ◆ The international kingdom of God in the Church

 **PLAY VIDEO**

Prayers Inspired by the Psalms

O Lord, I praise you!

Whether I am in your sanctuary or my parish,

going about my duties, or in the relaxation of nature,

I want to praise you with my life.

I remember your great help and works in my life;

You alone do I have to thank for my life and protection.

I praise you with my prayers,

my every breath reminds me of how great you are.

and I tell of your greatness to others.

Praises be to you!

(Adapted from Psalm 150)

"Here is one of the best means to acquire humility; fix well in mind this maxim: One is as much as he is in the sight of God, and no more."

— ST. FRANCIS OF ASSISI –

Review of Key Content

1. What are the two main themes of the Book of Psalms? How does the introductory drawing symbolize these two themes?

2. How many Psalms introduce the whole book of Psalms? What are the "two ways" one can choose to walk according to Psalm 1? Where do these two paths lead?

3. How is the "progression of sin" illustrated in Psalm 1? With what image is the "progression of sin" contrasted?

4. The Psalter uses personal experiences to instruct us in God's ways rather than legal precepts or commands. Whose experiences in particular are featured in the Psalms? What kind of experiences are found in the book?

5. Whose voice is heard by the psalmist in Psalm 2? In what two events in the Gospels can one hear echoes of Psalm 2?

6. What is the relationship between the Lord and David in Psalm 2? What is promised to David in Psalm 2?

Discussion Opportunities

(share thoughts with your group)

1. Reading Psalms becomes a vicarious experience of entering into the drama of David's life from its high points to its low points to everything in between. Recall a time when you confronted a spiritual challenge. How did you take that challenge or situation before God in prayer and live it according to God's will?

2. The Psalms instruct us in God's law, though not by presenting lists of rules and regulations. They also cover a broad range of spiritual, emotional, and physical circumstances, showing us that every situation in life can be brought before the Lord and made an opportunity for prayer. Have you encountered one that resonates with your own life that might help in your personal prayer?

3. Psalms 1-2 find their ultimate fulfillment in Christ, who is the Wisdom of God and the Royal Son of God. How might this affect the way you read the rest of the Book of Psalms? Does this change the way to look at the Old Testament as a Christian? Explain.

4. How does the image of the Catholic Church being the "international kingdom" of Jesus the King change your perspective on your obligations as a Catholic, such as Sunday Mass attendance, Confession, daily prayer?

Write Your Word Upon My Heart

"And Jesus came and said to them, 'All authority in heaven and on earth has been given to me. Go…make disciples of all nations.'"

MATTHEW 28:18-19

Notes & Journal

LESSON FIVE

Book I – David, the Suffering King

"The prayer of the People of God flourishes in the shadow of God's dwelling place, first the ark of the covenant and later the Temple."

CCC 2578

Review of Previous Lesson

Psalm 1 and 2 introduce the main themes of the Psalter, God's law and the royal son of David. Meditating on the Psalms immerses the reader in God's law (the first theme), and invites us to take refuge in God's Son, the Davidic Messiah (the second theme).

Psalm 1 presents the two paths of life: righteousness and wickedness. The first leads to salvation; the second to destruction. Progress in sin in the first lines of Psalm 1 contrasts immediately with meditation on God's law in the next lines. God's law (wisdom) in the mystic image of the tree of life (recalling Eden), helps overcome sin and grow in wisdom. Unlike the formal list of commands in the books of Moses, the Psalter instead contains prayers, songs, and praise. It offers instruction by way of illustration.

Psalm 2 presents us with the Messiah, who is both the royal Son of David and the Son of God. Using covenant language, it enunciates God's promise of worldwide kingship to the son of David. This second Psalm also invites us to follow the path of taking refuge in God's divine and royal Son, the descendant of David.

The path of meditating on wisdom (Psalm 1) and following the son of David (Psalm 2) become one path in the New Testament in the person of Jesus Christ.

Psalm 2 is one of the most important Psalms with regard to the New Testament. We hear this Psalm echoed at the Baptism and the Transfiguration of Christ when the voice of the Father announces, "This is my beloved Son in whom I am well pleased," which brings to mind Psalm 2:7.

Later on in Acts 4 we see the early Church taking up the words of Psalm 2 in prayer, and God shaking the house where they were and unleashing his great power in response.

In the light of the New Testament, the theology of Psalm 2, with its focus on the son of David as one who reigns over an international kingdom, brings into focus the theology of the *Church*. This understanding undergirds the messianic vision of the entire New Testament.

Topics Covered

- Main section of Book I – Psalm 1 through Psalm 41

- David's five responses in trouble
    1. Rejection of despair and continuing prayer in faith
    2. Remembrance of God's past deliverance
    3. Personal acts of faith: affirmation of faith in relationship with God (i.e., prayer, praise)
    4. Confession of sin, repentance, request for cleansing
    5. Praise of God in advance of his help

- Jesus' Quotations from Book I during His Passion
    - 41:9 *my bosom friend... has lifted his heel against me*
    - 22:1 *My God, my God, why have you abandoned me*
    - 31:5 *Into your hands, O Lord, I commend my spirit*
- Jesus' Teaching from Book I – Sermon on the Mount
    - 1st Beatitude: *Blessed are the poor in spirit* (King David)
    - 8th Beatitude: *Blessed are those who are persecuted* (King David)
    - *Blessed are the meek* – Ps 37:11 (*but the meek shall possess the land*)

- Five Psalms from Book I you need to know: 1, 2, 8, 22, 23

- Jesus' title Son of Man in Psalm 8

- Sacramental dimension of Psalm 23

 PLAY VIDEO

Prayers Inspired by the Psalms

I come to worship You, O Lord;

I am in awe of your might and holiness.

Within your temple, the Church, I make my plea.

Defend me against those who would lead me astray,

For I seek only to do your will through your steadfast love,

Your love which makes my way straight.

"Whether…we receive what we ask for, or do not receive it, let us still continue steadfast in prayer. For to fail in obtaining the desires of our heart, when God so wills it, is not worse than to receive it; for we know not as He does, what is profitable to us."

— ST. JOHN CHRYSOSTOM —

Review of Key Content

1. What are the three main causes of the many lament psalms in Book I of Psalms?

2. List some of the ways in which David responds to the causes of his suffering in the Psalms of Book I?

3. The video noted that Psalm 8—specifically its references to "man" and "the son of man"—could be interpreted along four different lines. Who are the four persons to whom Psalm 8 could be referring?

4. What specific sufferings of the Messiah are mentioned in Psalm 22? Is there any indication that Psalm 22 also looks beyond the agony of rejection and persecution to the joys of deliverance? Explain.

5. According to the video, sheep require attention because of their lack of intelligence. But they also have a notable quality that offers a lesson for us. What is the one great quality of sheep mentioned in Psalm 23?

6. Name the sacraments mentioned in Psalm 23.

Discussion Opportunities

(Share thoughts with your group)

1. Individual laments dominate Book I of the Psalms. Recall a time in your life that resembles some of the difficult situations in the Lament Psalms. Select three Book I Psalms which would have helped you. What specific helps are there?

2. David did not hide his fears, pains, and struggles from God. Just the opposite. In crisis or loss, David speaks his heart in prayer. How would you speak of the following to God:
- Your continuing faith in him
- Your experience of his saving graces in your life
- Your firm trust in him even now
- Your plea for forgiveness of your past sin

3. Have you ever "praised God in advance" for deliverance? What were the circumstances? Did God deliver you? Or, did God give you some other grace for which you are grateful?

Write Your Word Upon My Heart

"In thy strength the king rejoices, O LORD; and in thy help how greatly he exults!...For the king trusts in the LORD; and through the streadfast love of the Most High he shall not be moved."

PSALM 21:1, 7

Notes & Journal

LESSON SIX

Book II – The Glory of Zion, David's City

"The prayer of the People of God flourished in the shadow of the dwelling place of God's presence on earth, the ark of the covenant and the Temple, under the guidance of their shepherds, especially King David...."

CCC 2594

Review of Previous Lesson

Book I of the Psalter, which extends from Psalm 1–41, has a large concentration of individual laments. David's prayers here are dominated by the pressure, stress, and duress he feels from various causes: illness, his own sins, his enemies.

David responds to these causes of suffering in five ways:

1. David does not despair, he keeps his faith in God and continues to pray and speak to Him.
2. Using his memories, David speaks of God's mighty deeds in the past, especially God's deliverance of David himself.
3. David makes verbal acts of faith and trust to God.
4. David confesses his sins, seeing them as one of the causes of his affliction.
5. David praises God in advance of God coming to his rescue.

From these Psalms of lament, Jesus draws many of His teachings and prayers in the Gospels.

- In Psalm 22:1, Jesus prays from the Cross: *My God, my God, why have you forsaken me?*
- Some of the Beatitudes in the Sermon on the Mount are indebted to Book I of Psalms.
- Three important Psalms from Book I are Psalms 8, 22, 23.

Psalm 8: *O Lord, our Lord, how majestic is your name in all the earth!*

- Key understanding: Jesus, who calls himself the Son of Man, sees himself as the King of creation....*what is man that you are mindful of him, and **the son of man**, that you care for him?*
- Four possible understandings of *man* in this Psalm: Adam, David, everyman, Messiah.

Psalm 22: *My God, my God, why have you forsaken me?* (a *todah* psalm)

- Multiple links with the Crucifixion
- Verse 23: *You who fear the Lord, praise him!*
- Psalm ending: triumph and deliverance
- Jesus' prophecy: ultimate victory of God

Psalm 23: *The Lord is my shepherd; I shall not want*

- Lord as Shepherd of sheep
- Sheep as unintelligent, needy, vulnerable, loyal
- Followers of a shepherd voice
- Psalm beloved by the Church Fathers as sacramental instruction
- Eucharistic references
- "Catholic" Psalm

Topics Covered

- ◆ David's Liturgical Reform
  1. Appointment of a levitical choir of the sons of Korah and a choir leader Asaph
  2. Establishment of the *todah*, or thanksgiving praise, as more important than burnt offerings
  3. Specific prayer for eternal legacy of David through Solomon, ultimately to the Messiah
- ◆ Overview of Book II: Psalms 42-72
  - Psalm 45: Royal Wedding foreshadowing Christ as Bridegroom
  - Psalm 46-48: Zion Psalms praise David's City as the Lord's glorious dwelling
  - Psalms 50: written by Asaph, a choir leader appointed by David
  - Psalms 51-64: look back on David's early years, his deliverance from foes
  - Psalms 65-68: praises of God's salvation for David
  - Psalms 69-71: prayers for preservation of David's testimony to God in future generations

- Book II contrast to Book I: twice the number of Psalms end in praise in Book II.
- Five Psalms from Book II
  - Psalm 45: Royal Wedding Psalm: voice of court minstrel and the bride, Marian imagery, prophecy of divinity of Christ
  - Psalm 46: praise of God for Jerusalem, sign of God as refuge, allusion to water spring as image of Holy Spirit
  - Psalm 50: *Todah*, the sacrifice of thanksgiving that God really wants, foreshadows the Eucharist
  - Psalm 51: *Miserere* Psalm, theology of repentance, confession, original sin, gift of Holy Spirit
  - Psalm 72: high point of Psalms before Book V, glories of Solomon's reign, prophecy of Jesus' ministry

Prayers Inspired by the Psalms

You, God, are my Lord and Savior.

It is you alone whom I trust.

When I come to you in your tabernacle in prayer,

I hear your call to rest only in you and your protection.

You are the rock upon whom I shall lean,

You are the salvation in which I shall trust.

While I kneel before you, undisturbed by anything,

You offer me your own glory; in your glory is my safety

(Adapted from Psalm 62)

Let no worldly prosperity divert you, nor any worldly adversity restrain you, from His praise.

— ST ANSELM OF CANTERBURY —

Review of Key Content

1. King David is considered a liturgical reformer of Israel's sanctuary worship. Name two important changes he initiated.

2. Psalm 45 describes the joy and pageantry of a royal wedding. What figures of the New Testament are foreshowed in this scene? What is said of the king that is only literally true of Jesus Christ?

3. What is the message of Psalm 50 on the subject of sacrifices in relation to God? What is being denied? What kind of sacrifice does the Lord ultimately want?

4. Psalm 46 mentions the river that makes glad the city of God. What is this a reference to? What does its name suggest about the way Israel viewed Jerusalem? What does this life-giving spring ultimately signify?

5. What are two significant differences between the burnt offering and the thank offering in Temple worship mentioned in this lesson?

6. What Psalm is reserved for Fridays in the prayers of the Church? Why? What important Christian truths does this psalm touch upon?

Discussion Opportunities

(share thoughts with your group)

1. In the Royal Wedding Psalm, the bride promises she will give the king heirs to perpetuate his name and legacy. What does Israel want to remember about David's name or legacy? Is there someone in your extended family whose name or legacy you (or your family) want to remember?

2. When a *todah* offering was made in thanksgiving for God's deliverance of the psalmist from some danger or distress, part of the sacrificial animal was eaten with festal joy. What might that suggest about the Eucharist? What should be the disposition of our hearts when we partake of the offering? What deliverance do Christians celebrate with festal joy?

3. The *Miserere* (Psalm 51) is a significant part of Lent and of Friday Liturgy of the Hours. How do you speak to God when you recognize your need for repentance? What response do you want or expect from Him in return? What does Psalm 51 suggest about our proper response to God when sins are committed?

4. Psalm 72 is understood as fulfilling God's promise to bless the nations in Abraham. One can see a preliminary fulfillment of this during the reign of Solomon, who shared his wisdom with the world. Where do you see the blessings of God's Wisdom (the Holy Spirit) in your life as a descendant of Abraham? Are there any sacraments in particular where this blessing is conferred?

5. Blessed Holy Water and blessed oil are sacramentals available for the faithful and are signs of the Holy Spirit's cleansing and blessing. When might you want to use these?

6. Psalm 45:9 *...at your right hand stands the queen in gold of Ophir.* Catholic Mariology tells us that this refers to Mary, the Blessed Mother of Jesus. How might this verse encourage you to address her as Queen? What might you like to say to her as Jesus' Queen?

Write Your Word Upon My Heart

"...[T]he faithful will abide with him in love, because grace and mercy are upon his elect, and he watches over his holy ones."

WISDOM 3:9

Notes & Journal

LESSON SEVEN

Book III – The Collapse of the Kingdom of David

"...although the Lord shows patience for the sake of his name, the people turn away from the Holy One of Israel and profane his name among the nations."

CCC 2811

Review of Previous Lesson

More joyful than Book I, Book II begins with Psalm 42, the first Psalm authored by the sons of Korah, a choir of Levites appointed by David, who was a great liturgical reformer. Preceded by two laments, Psalm 45 shifts the mood to joy in the Royal Wedding Psalm, which foreshadows Christ the Bridegroom. The next three Psalms, 46-48, the Zion Psalms, sing of Jerusalem, Israel's capital, at the height of its glory during the reigns of David and Solomon.

Asaph, the man appointed by David to lead the liturgical choir, authors the next Psalm (50). Then, Psalms 51-64 retell the story of David's early years, specifically how God delivered David. Psalms 65-68 follow, joyfully celebrating the salvation given to David by God.

Psalms 69 through 71 are probably from David's later years, when David pleads with God: *do not forsake me till I proclaim your might to all the generations to come*. David asks God to allow him to testify about God to future generations. Finally, Psalm 72 calls on God to bless Solomon, David's son and heir. In 1 Kings 4 Solomon's reign describes how God did indeed answer David's plea.

Five specific Psalms (45, 46, 50, 51, 72) stand out in Book II. Psalm 45, the Royal Wedding Psalm, written for one of Solomon's weddings, gives the words of a court minstrel, who describes the joy of those at the wedding. It also addresses the bride, and the bride herself speaks her promise to the king: She will provide him heirs who will tell his name to future generations, perpetuating his legacy. This Psalm prepares for Mary's coronation, the wedding parables of Jesus, and the miracle of wine in John 2.

Psalm 46, a Zion Psalm, praises the holy city Jerusalem as a sign of God's refuge for Jacob (Israel). Its allusion to the spring of water in Jerusalem, named Gihon, evokes the idea of a sacred river, seen in Eden and Jerusalem, at the Cross from the side of Christ, and in the Book of Revelation ("the River of Life"). This spring is the Holy Spirit.

Psalm 50 (first Psalm of Asaph) presents the superiority of the *todah* to the "burnt offering," an animal sacrifice to atone for sin. The *todah* was a thanksgiving sacrifice, offered for an act of deliverance which God had provided.

Psalm 51, the *Miserere*, makes the important theological point that all sin is an offence against God and requires repentance and reconciliation to God, in addition to our neighbor. The verse, *In sin my mother conceived me. I was brought forth in iniquity*, lays essential groundwork for the doctrine of original sin.

Psalm 72 marks the high point of the Psalms (until Book V), a prayer about Solomon that David prays for his son. It describes the glories of Solomon's reign, an early realization of God's promise to bless all the nations through Abraham's offspring. It also prophesies the life and ministry of our Lord Jesus.

Topics Covered

David and Solomon's kingdom decays and becomes dissolute. Psalm 73 begins Book III with worry about the prosperity of the wicked. Psalm 74 describes the destruction of the Temple. Book III contains the largest collection of communal laments of the entire Psalter (74, 77, 79, 80, 83, 85, 89). In Psalm 81, God rebukes Israel for its sin. Psalm 88 ends with *my companions are in darkness*. Psalm 88 has become a common prayer of pilgrims traveling to where Jesus was jailed when he was arrested in Israel. Psalm 89 mourns in verse 39: *Yet you have renounced and spurned and been enraged at your anointed* ("christ"), though it does present the promises of the Davidic covenant, especially universal rule of the king.

• Psalm 73: *Truly God is good to the upright....But...my feet...almost stumbled.*
  • Perennial struggle: why do the evil prosper and the good suffer?
  • Verses 16-17: Psalmist reaches understanding in the midst of worship
  • Mass (worship): our re-orientation to divine perspective on reality.

- Psalm 81: *O that my people would listen to me, that Israel would walk in my ways!*
  - Perennial call to repentance and conversion; all sin turns the sinner away from God.
  - Anticipations of Sacraments of Reconciliation and the Eucharist
  - Most severe punishment from God: giving us what we want, rather than Himself

- Psalm 84: *O Lord of hosts, blessed is the man who trusts in you.*
  - Worship brings consolation on the journey through the valley of tears
  - *Courts of the Lord* (the act of worship) bring consolation and right understanding

- Psalm 88: *I am reckoned among those who go down to the Pit*
  - Ending includes no indication of hope.
  - Psalms invite us to be brutally honest and transparent with the Lord in prayer
  - Even in times of darkness, continuing a dialogue with the Lord is an act of faith

- Psalm 89: *I will sing of your mercy...forever – you renounced the covenant with your servant*
  - Details the parameters of the Davidic covenant.
  - Sorrowful ending: pointer toward the coming of Christ

Prayers Inspired by the Psalms

Lord, I know your promise to the upright.

Yet the arrogant prosper, increasing their wealth,

without care. Do you know of their wickedness?

I sigh with suffering, finding it too difficult to bear.

I come into Your Presence to speak to you. There, you say

quietly, their deeds will be punished forever, while I will be

with Your glory regardless of my earthly distress.

Stay in my heart, O Lord; You yourself are my eternal portion.

(Adapted from Psalm 73)

"God wishes us not to rest upon anything but His infinite goodness; do not let us expect anything, hope anything, or desire anything but from Him, and let us put our trust and confidence in Him alone."

— ST. CHARLES BORROMEO —

Review of Key Content

1. How is Psalm 73 different from Psalm 72, the final psalm of Book II? What does Asaph lament of in Psalm 73 at the beginning of Book III? How common is the struggle he faces?

2. Where does Asaph turn to find an answer to his questions and to see things from God's perspective ?

3. What tragic event is described in Psalm 74? How does this contribute to the mood of Book III?

4. Name the three lessons about prayer that one can find in Psalm 88.

5. What does Psalm 89 have to say about the Davidic covenant? How do God's promises to David contrast with the ending of the psalm?

6. How is Psalm 89 related to the liturgical feast of Christ the King?

Discussion Opportunities

(share thoughts with your group)

1. In the opening psalm of Book III, Asaph worries about the worldly success of the "arrogant" and seems to wrestle with a bit of jealousy. Have you experienced a situation when worry and observation of others' arrogance and success troubled your spiritual life (or another's)?

2. The turning point in Psalm 73 comes when Aspah says: *until I went into the sanctuary of God; then I perceived their end.* Explain what happened to Asaph. What experiences in adoration have moved you to conversion, or what experiences in prayer have shown you how to approach struggles or problems differently? How can prayer widen your perspective and help you to see things in a different light?

3. In Psalm 81, God addresses Israel, saying *O that my people would listen to me, that Israel would walk in my ways! I would soon subdue their enemies....I would feed you with the finest of wheat.* Can you think of a bad situation in your own life that dramatically improved after you made a concerted effort at prayer and deeper conversion?

4. The sons of Korah sing of the joys that come with being in the Lord's sanctuary: *How lovely is your dwelling place, O Lord of Hosts!...my heart and my flesh sing for joy to the living God.* Relate an experience in your life when worshiping in the Lord's presence filled you with spiritual joy. What would you say to skeptics who claim that prayer and praise are merely crutches in a cruel world?

5. In Psalm 88, the psalmist complains openly that God seems to have abandoned him, doesn't answer his prayers, and has taken even human friendship from him. Yet he keeps calling out to God. He keeps the channels of communication with God open. Has this ever happened to you or to someone you know? What benefit does this kind of prayer have in times when God feels distant and disinterested in your struggles?

6. Psalm 89 begins: *I will sing of your mercy, O Lord, forever; with my mouth I will proclaim your faithfulness to all generations.* What are some of the mercies of God that you've experienced in your own life?

Write Your Word Upon My Heart

"My soul magnifies the Lord, and my spirit rejoices in God my Savior."

LUKE 1:46-47

Notes & Journal

LESSON EIGHT

Book IV – Israel in Exile

"The words of the Psalmist, sung for God, both express and acclaim the Lord's saving works; the same Spirit inspires both God's work and man's response."

CCC 2587

Review of Previous Lesson

In contrast to Book II, the glory of the kingdom of David, Book III shows the kingdom of Solomon's decay and dissolution. Psalm 73 begins with Asaph the author struggling with the prosperity of the wicked and the oppression of the righteous. He mentions even his own jealousy and his near fall into being one of the wicked. Psalm 74 continues in sharp contrast to Psalm 72, speaking about enemies of God's people destroying the Temple.

Book III contains the largest number of communal laments of the whole Psalter (74, 77, 79, 80, 82, 83, 89). These arise out of situations of national distress and harassment by enemies. Psalm 78 details the unfaithfulness of Israel in biblical history. Psalm 81, unique in the Psalter, presents the words of God rebuking Israel for idolatry. This book's dark tone follows the dissolution of the kingdom of David and Solomon over centuries. Often said when pilgrims visit the cistern where Jesus was held after His arrest, Psalm 88 presents no hope, ending with the words: *my companions are the darkness.* Though Psalm 89 starts with: *I will sing of your mercies, O Lord, forever*, it breaks at verse 38 with: *you have renounced the covenant with your servant.* The psalmist watches the king, probably Zedekiah in 587 BC, being blinded and dragged off in chains to Babylon to die in exile.

Five Psalms represent the highlights of Book III: Psalms 73, 81, 84, 88, and 89. Most important is the last exhortation in Psalm 89 where the Psalmist refuses to give up praying and proclaiming: *I will proclaim your faithfulness to all generations.* The latter part of Psalm 89 laments the humiliation of Israel's Davidic kings, though it still ends with the obligatory Psalm wording: *blessed be the Lord forever. Amen and amen.* A very clear description of the Davidic covenant is in Psalm 89: the king is the son of God, ruling over all the earth on a throne that God swore would stand forever. In this respect, Psalm 89 points forward to the everlasting reign of Christ the King. Christ is the ultimate answer to all the cries and laments of Book III.

Topics Covered

Book IV responds to exile and loss. Psalm 90 (prayer of Moses) returns to the Mosaic covenant for understanding, reminding Israel that God is the true dwelling of man, his everlasting refuge. Psalm 105 reviews the course of salvation history and Psalm 106 recounts Israel's continued unfaithfulness to the covenant. These two psalms work together to highlight an important truth: though Israel was exiled because of unfaithfulness, God is faithful. Israel contemplates this reality far away from the Promised Land in the lands of captivity. Book IV concludes by asking the Lord to save his people from their exile among nations.

• Themes of Book IV
   1. The Lord is a dwelling place for his people, whether or not there's a Temple in Jerusalem
   2. The Lord is King, whether or not there's a king in Jerusalem
   3. The Lord shows his glory throughout the world in creation
   4. The Lord's goodness and mercy invite us to give thanks

• Moses' prayerful advice in Psalm 90
   1. Jerusalem is lost, but remember that God is our proper dwelling.
   2. Life is short, so ask God to teach you wisdom for living.
   3. Life is dominated by labor, so ask God to establish the work of your hands.

• Psalm 90: the one psalm attributed to Moses. God is our dwelling place, ask God for wisdom to make the most of your days, ask God to make your labor here last for eternity.

• Psalm 91: a psalm of spiritual warfare. Real shelter, security, safety come only from God. In our Catholic tradition, this psalm is approved for the rite of exorcism and contributes to the doctrine of guardian angels.

• Psalm 95: a call to worship, used daily in the Liturgy of the Hours to speak of God's goodness and compassion.

- Psalm 100: a psalm described as "for the thank offering", which in Hebrew is the *todah*. God's people sing of his goodness and covenant faithfulness.

- Psalm 104: Reflection on God's glory in creation and his blessing on all the earth's creatures. When you send forth your spirit, they are created and you renew the face of the earth.

 **PLAY VIDEO**

Prayers Inspired by the Psalms

Praise God, O my heart,

May those who pray with me praise the Lord.

for You, LORD, are God, my Maker, my Shepherd.

I thank You for your kindness and mercy;

I thank you that I belong to you in Your faithfulness

and Your mercy. Soften my heart, Lord,

that I may worship you rightly

and follow Your way.

Amen.

(Adapted from Book IV of the Psalms)

"The more we are afflicted in this world, the greater is our assurance in the next; the more sorrow in the present, the greater will be our joy in the future."

— ST ISIDORE OF SEVILLE —

Review of Key Content

1. What advice does Moses give to the exiles of Israel? How are his words related to Israel's loss of the Temple and banishment from the Promised Land?

2. Explain the last verse of Psalm 90: *Let the favor of the Lord our God be upon us, and establish thou the work of our hands upon us, yea, the work of our hands establish thou it.*

3. Book IV insists that the Lord is the only true God. How would this message resonate with God's people in exile? If the pagans all around them don't worship the Lord, then what do they really worship?

4. Name four leading themes of Book IV of Psalms.

5. Psalm 95 tells us why we should worship God. List and explain the attributes of God that it singles out for praise.

6. Psalm 140 is featured in the Easter Vigil liturgy and again in the liturgy for Pentecost? What is significant about this? What is the message of verse 30 in particular?

7. One of the Psalms in Book IV is approved for the Catholic rite of exorcism. Which one? What makes this psalm appropriate for such a setting?

Discussion Opportunities

(share thoughts with your group)

1. Imagine being separated from your house of worship and your homeland. Many refugees in history have experienced this. Imagine further that you're a captive detained against your will. To what Catholic practices would you turn for comfort or to keep you faithful to God?

2. What motivates your work? Do you labor to care for a family, to attain an ideal, to fulfill a sense of duty? Does it matter to you whether your work lasts? If so, what from your labors do you want God to preserve for the future?

3. In spite of the failures, broken relationships, and sins in your life, where do you experience God's faithfulness to you? Are you in the habit of thanking God for being faithful, even when you're not? Have you turned to God for help in difficult situations?

4. Can you think of a human institution or organization that has disappointed you? What is your reaction when it does? What help does God offer in those challenges?

5. Select a psalm that praises God for his creation from Book IV. What specific aspects of creation move you to prayer, especially the prayers of adoration and thanksgiving?

6. What Christian songs or Catholic hymns are your favorites and why? Are you more attracted to songs of praise, encouragement, or worship? Why?

7. What's your relationship with the Holy Spirit like? Is the third Person of the Trinity neglected in your spiritual life, or do you seek the Spirit's help often? How do you pray to the Holy Spirit?

Write Your Word Upon My Heart

"I will heal their faithlessness; I will love them freely, for my anger has turned from them....They shall return and dwell beneath my shadow, they shall flourish as a garden; they shall blossom as the vine, their fragrance shall be like the wine of Lebanon."

HOSEA 14:4,7

Notes & Journal

LESSON NINE

Book V – Israel's Return and Restoration

"Prayed and fulfilled in Christ, the Psalms are an essential and permanent element of the prayer of the Church. They are suitable for men of every condition and time."

CCC 2597

Review of Previous Lesson

Book IV is a response to the decline and fall of the Davidic kingdom. The covenant appears to be broken, the kingdom has been destroyed, and the people taken away from their homeland. Psalms in Book IV look back to the covenant before the Davidic covenant for answers to these calamities. They turn first to Moses.

Psalm 90 presents us with Moses' advice and comfort as Israel tries to understand the loss of their dwelling in Jerusalem. Moses urges them: (1) to see that only God is our true dwelling place, (2) to recognize how short life is, which means that our time of suffering is also short; and (3) to call on God for help in establishing the work of their hands, making it meaningful for future generations.

By the end of Book IV, Psalms 105 and 106 give a review of salvation history, providing the answer to the question, "Why are we in exile?" The reason is not because God was unfaithful, but because the Israelites weren't true to God.

Themes in Book IV: God as dwelling place, true King and only true God, God's glory in creation, learning to sing a new song to God. At the conclusion of the book, the restoration of Israel also becomes a theme.

Psalm 90: *Lord, thou hast been our dwelling place in all generations.*

• Though Jerusalem is lost, God is our dwelling.

• Life is short and so is the suffering in it.

• Pray that God will make your labor last.

Psalm 91: *His faithfulness is a shield and buckler. You will not fear the terror of the night…*

• Often used in spiritual warfare for protection and approved for formal rite of exorcism

• Contributes to the Catholic doctrine of guardian angels

• Attributed to Solomon and used in times of affliction

Psalm 95: *O that today you would hearken to his voice! Harden not your hearts….*

• Favorite call to worship in the Psalter, used for Lauds (morning prayer) in the Liturgy of the Hours

• A message of God's greatness and power demonstrated in creation

• Extols God's goodness and compassion towards creation and humanity

Psalm 100: *Enter his gates with thanksgiving,…Give thanks to him, bless his name.*

• Only Psalm with a title designating it for the thank offering (*todah*), which is a precursor of the Eucharist

• Often set to familiar tune known as "Old Hundredth"

• A thanksgiving for God's goodness, creation, and enduring mercy

Psalm 104: *When you send forth your Spirit, they are created;…you renew the face of the earth.*

• Reflects on beauty of God's love displayed in creation and forms background for some of Jesus' teaching

• Used as responsorial during Easter Season of the liturgical year

• A call to praise God as creator of universe and of the Church

Topics Covered

Book V, covering Psalms 107–150, is the grand finale of the Psalter. It resonates with themes of joy and thanksgiving as it celebrates the experience of God's people returning from exile, rebuilding the Temple, and reestablishing themselves in the land of Israel. It brings the entire collection of biblical psalms to a crescendo of praise.

Among the various collections within this final book, we should note the Egyptian Hallel Psalms, which were sung at Passover (Ps 113–118), the Psalms of Ascent, which were sung when Jews traveled to worship God in his Temple in Jerusalem (Ps 120–134), and the Hallelujah Collection, which conclude the Psalter by inviting all creatures to form a chorus of praise (Ps 146–150). Dr. Bergsma singles out five psalms that are important to become familiar with:

Psalm 110: *The Lord said to my lord, sit at my right hand, til I make your enemies your footstool.*

- God speaking to the king, divine promise to defeat the king's enemies

- God's fatherhood of the Davidic Son from the beginning of time.

- Ultimately fulfilled in Christ, the Davidic king and Melchizedekian priest of the New Covenant.

Psalm 118: *This is the day that the Lord has made; let us rejoice and be glad in it. Todah* – a Psalm recited in the Temple, thanking God for a specific act of deliverance

- Prayed by Jesus and the apostles on the night of the Last Supper

- Prayed by the Church in connection with the Passion and Resurrection of Jesus

Psalm 119: *Blessed are those whose way is blameless, who walk in the law of the Lord!*

- Effusive praise for the blessings of God's Law

- Seven synonyms for God's law: word, promise, commandment, statute, ordinance, testimony, precept

- Acrostic Psalm using the Hebrew alphabet from first, *aleph* (A), to last, *tav* (T)

Psalm 136: *O, give thanks to the Lord, for He is good, for His mercy endures forever.*

- Probably a Temple litany led with response for *His mercy endures forever*

- God is worthy of praise because of His Goodness and everlasting mercy (*hesed*)

- Major theme of entire Psalter: God's goodness in Himself, and His mercy to us

Psalm 150: *Let everything that breathes praise the LORD!*

- Praise of God not only with voices but with musical instruments

- Praise of God not only by men and women but by all creatures great and small

 **PLAY VIDEO**

Prayers Inspired by the Psalms

You, Lord, are my deliverer, and I live only in your shadow.
You send help from angels against enemies, disease, and terror.
Though others are tormented and fall, I seek refuge in you
in prayer and contemplation. I lift my eyes to You,
and pay no attention to the threats beneath my feet.
O guardians of the Lord, lift me up to my Savior God.
Amen.
(Adapted from Psalm 91)

"Yes, a psalm is a blessing on the lips of the people, praise of God, the assembly's homage…."

— ST AMBROSE OF MILAN —

Review of Key Content

1. Name three liturgical celebrations in the Church that use psalms from Book V. How do these psalms relate to the events celebrated?

2. What Psalms were sung by ancient Jews as they walked to Jerusalem to worship the Lord in the Temple?

3. What are the two collections of David's Psalms in Book V?

4. What command stands out as the recurring refrain of Psalms 146–150? What is that command? What does it mean?

5. Psalm 110 presents words spoken by the Lord to the Davidic king. What does he promise to do for the king? What other sacred office is entrusted to this king?

6. Which of the psalms in Book V may have originally formed the ending of the book? What is its main focus, and how does this relate to Psalm 1?

7. Which of the psalms in Book V reads like a litany in which a priest or Levite proclaims something praiseworthy about God and the assembly responds with a refrain? What is that famous refrain?

8. What tips does Dr. Bergsma offer to make the Psalms a part of your prayer life?

Discussion Opportunities

(share thoughts with your group)

1. Several times Book V seems to stop and then start again in full-throated praise of God. When have you experienced in prayer, or together with others in prayer, that need to continue praising God for favors in your life or favors in the life of your spiritual community?

2. Psalms 113 through 118 were chanted as hymns during the Israelite celebration of Passover. Do you and your family sing songs on liturgical feast days, (e.g., Christmas carols and Easter hymns).

3. Throughout Book V, the psalmists invite Israel to review their history with God. The people are urged to praise God for His power and goodness, to ask forgiveness for sin, to celebrate deliverance, and to worship Him for His mercy and salvation (which will come ultimately with the promised Messiah). Compare these commands from the Psalmist with the celebration of the Liturgical Year from Advent through Christmas, Lent through Easter and Ordinary Time. How are we invited to do similar things in our relationship with God?

4. Name one spiritual benefit you have received while studying the Psalms in these videos and with the companion workbook. Write in your notes for Lesson 9 what new habit of prayer through the Psalms you will begin on your spiritual journey toward God.

Write Your Word Upon My Heart

"Praise the Lord! Praise God in his sanctuary; praise him in his mighty firmament! Praise him for his mighty deeds; praise his according to his exceeding greatness!"

Psalm 150:1-2

Notes & Journal

Want more spiritual nourishment?

Check out **The Art of Catholic podcast**. Available on Youtube, iTunes, Spotify, Stitcher, and more!

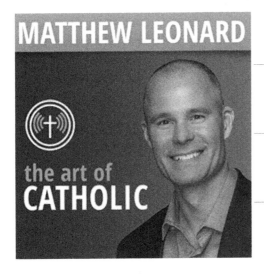

Pocast Heaven ★★★★★
by Trevor-Fooling

Awesome. ★★★★★
by Harleypierrepont

Truth BOMB ★★★★★
by BC Raven 44

Out. Of. The. Park. ★★★★★
by Bobby McQuin

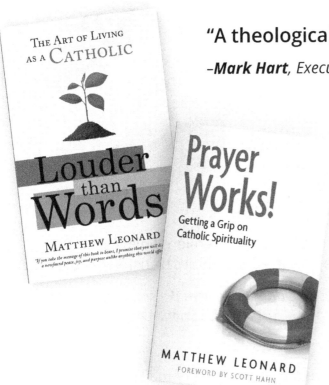

"A theological thrill ride!"

–*Mark Hart*, *Executive Vice-President of LifeTeen International*

"Matthew Leonard has a knack for crisp and clear expression that virtually anyone can understand. Add to this a sprinkle of memorable stories and a great sense of humor and you've got yourself a rare find."

–*Curtis Mitch*, *Author of the Ignatius Catholic Study Bible*

How About A Powerful Video Study That Will Actually Change Your Life?

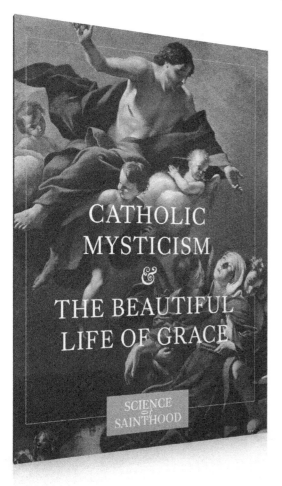

Catholic Mysticism & the Beautiful Life of Grace

In the Gospel of Luke, Jesus says that only "one thing" is necessary...the interior life. And once you really understand what He's talking about, everything changes!

In a series of 15 powerful presentations, renowned teacher Matthew Leonard dives into the rich, mystical tradition of Catholic spirituality in a way you've never heard before.

Catholic Mysticism & the Beautiful Life of Grace is a portion of the popular Science of Sainthood series from Next Level Catholic Academy. It's a series that has touched the lives of thousands of Catholics from around the world.

"Deeply penetrating!"

"SO POWERFUL. I've never in all my life gotten such clear training on spiritual growth!"

"I will watch it over and over..."

"More than education, this is *transformation*!"

Available for both group and individual study.
Bulk discounts on workbooks are available.

Learn more at NextLevelCatholicAcademy.com.

41206150R00044